Debra enjoys dancing, deep sea fishing, golf, the beach, traveling, and reading.

*Contact:*
(786) 262-9991
djohnsonking@gmail.com

We Need To Talk
About...

# H.I.T.S.S.

## HEAD IN THE SAND SYNDROME

DEBRA L. JOHNSON-KING

Copyright © 2022 by Debra L. Johnson-King.

ISBN 978-1-64133-692-5 (softcover)
ISBN 978-1-64133-693-2 (ebook)

All rights reserved. No part of this book may be reproduced or transmitted in any form or by any means, electronic or mechanical, including photocopying, recording, or by any information storage and retrieval system without express written permission from the author, except in the case of brief quotations embodied in critical reviews and certain other noncommercial uses permitted by copyright law.

Printed in the United States of America.

Brilliant Books Literary
137 Forest Park Lane Thomasville
North Carolina 27360 USA

# ABOUT THE AUTHOR

## *Debra L. Johnson-King*

Debra L. Johnson-King is a Financial Strategist/Coach and the Founder & CEO of The DebJon Group (Your Financial Concierge), a "boutique" financial services company, which provides financial education and planning to individuals and companies by matching clients with the right financial products and services. Additionally, she is the Community Development Manager for a major nationwide lender.

Debra has a breadth of experience that is not very common in the industry having worked in many segments of the financial arena: from mortgage loan origination to life insurance and annuities, income tax preparation, credit and bankruptcy counseling, HUD certified housing counselor, licensed real estate agent, and certified debt eliminator. Additionally, Debra is a sought-after speaker and writer.

Additionally, Debra is a board member of The Bankrate Financial Review Board of Bankrate Magazine and is a member of numerous civic and professional organizations such as the Mortgage Bankers Association, Florida Association of Mortgage Professionals, and NAR (National Association of Realtors) to name a few.

For over 20 years, Debra has given financial wellness presentations to thousands of individuals, organizations, churches, and corporations across the country and around the world, advising them on how to better their financial situations, grow wealth, develop multiple streams of income, break the mental chains of debt, and eliminate their dysfunctional relationship with money.

# H.I.T.S.S.

## (HEAD IN THE SAND SYNDROME)

## By Debra L. Johnson-King

The Head in the Sand is synonymous/ parallels the perceived behavior of the ostrich. Contrary to popular belief, ostriches <u>do not</u> bury their heads in the sand. When an ostrich senses danger and cannot run away, it flops to the ground and remains still, thereby giving/ creating that illusion. **Pliny the Elder,** a Roman author, naturalist and natural philosopher who lived 23 AD–79 AD, wrote that ostriches "imagine when they have thrust their head and neck onto a bush that the whole of their body is concealed."

Head in The Sand Syndrome or H.I.T.S.S. is a combination of complex human behaviors. It encompasses avoidance behavior, denial, procrastination, fear, embarrassment, and depression. We condition ourselves to believe that as long as we don't deal with the situation at hand, as long as we don't acknowledge the situation, it will cease to exist, or go away, or not get any worse. Thus the H.I.T.S.S. theory was born.

Are you afraid to answer the telephone? Does the sound of the ringer strike terror in your heart? Does the sight of an unknown number on the caller ID cause your heart to go into overdrive? Mail arrives and what do you do with it? It's piled high unopened on the kitchen counter or thrust deep into the bottom drawer, there to remain unopened forever, willingly applying the old adage, "Out of sight, out of mind."

The first step to solving/curing any problem is to recognize and acknowledge that one exists. This step is **HUGE!** The whole premise of H.I.T.S.S. is **not** dealing with problems, and/or acting like they do not exist.

Let us examine in more detail some of the types of behavior displayed by people suffering from H.I.T.S.S. syndrome.

1. **Avoidance**—In exhibiting this type of behavior one keeps away from, prevents from happening, does not do, let alone a situation.
2. **Denial**—In exhibiting this type of behavior, one has a disbelief in the existence or reality of a situation/thing. An outright refusal to recognize or acknowledge a situation.
3. **Procrastination**—In exhibiting this type of behavior, one defers taking action, delays, puts off till another day or time.
4. **Fear**—In exhibiting this type of behavior, one has feelings of being afraid, whether the threat is real or imagined.
5. **Embarrassment**—In exhibiting this type of behavior, one feels confusion and shame and even discomfort.
6. **Depression**—In exhibiting this type of behavior, one shows signs of general emotional withdrawal, also great sadness.

What is the problem/situation that is causing you to exhibit H.I.T.S.S. behavior?

1. A relationship
2. Loss of a job
3. Loss of a loved one
4. Loss (losing) your home
5. Battling health issues
6. Addiction
7. Overwhelming financial debt

## 1. A relationship

This covers a broad spectrum of connectedness between people; a state of involving mutual dealings between people. For example, there exist relationships between you and your significant other, you and your children, you and your siblings, you and your parents, you and your boss (to name a few). In relationships boundaries have to be set and followed. No-one but you can determine how you are treated, lines in the sand have to be drawn and not allowed to be crossed. Let's take a closer look at some of these relationships.

a) You and your significant other: You realize that things have not been quite the

## 2. Loss of a Job

In these trying economic times downsizing and layoffs are common. So, you'd been on your job for a number of years and got laid off. Guess what? So have millions of other people. Having a pity party and laying home on the couch is not going to pay the bills. You've sent out dozens of resumes for jobs in your field/line of work. Employers say that you are overqualified for the positions. Or they 'insult' you by offering you positions way below your capabilities and paying much less than you are accustomed to making. In your mind, it costs you more to go to work than to stay at home for that salary! And the bills keep piling up. It's time to get off the couch. Start looking at and applying for positions in other fields. Look at perhaps turning your hobby into a business. What is it that you are good at?

A client was laid off from her job of over 20 years. Whilst employed, she baked cakes and sold them to friends and family. She was self-taught (trial and error) and by watching YouTube videos. After being laid off, she took classes in baking at a local community college, Additionally, she got a job at a bakery to learn the real world aspect of being a baker and running a business. She has partnered with a party planner/caterer and together they run a successful catering business.

Re-invent yourself. Train for a different career. Start attending free workshops and seminars. Get out and network. Call every person that you have ever met and let them know that you are looking for work. Re-do your resume, focus on different areas than before. Now is not the time to be embarrassed. Closed mouths do not get fed.

**TAKE YOUR HEAD OUT THE SAND!**

## 3. Loss of a Loved one

Perhaps a parent, a child, a spouse, someone close to you has died. They were taken from you through sickness, tragedy, or just natural causes. No one could possibly know the pain that you feel. Some days it's so unbearable you feel like you can't go on. You have been grieving excessively to the exclusion of others in your life. You perhaps have other children that you are neglecting. Other relationships that have deteriorated or even been destroyed because of your lack of interest and participation in them. The person who is no longer there still occupies and remains the focal point of your world.

Mrs. B was a referral from a previous client. As she entered the office grief and depression oozed from her pores. Her whole countenance was one of defeat and profound sadness. In each hand was a grocery bag. Her husband of over 50 years, her childhood sweetheart, had passed away. They never had children and she was all alone. She didn't drive and had never worked a day in her life. He had taken care of everything, and she did not have a clue about anything. Now she was all alone. Her house was in foreclosure, with a sale date already set. I usually do not mix religion with business in the office, but I was moved to ask if she minded if we prayed before we got started. She replied that she would welcome prayer. So we prayed.

During the course of the consultation, I discovered that the grocery bags were full of unopened mail from her lender. They had made numerous attempts to contact her. As well as numerous resolutions offered, but she was paralyzed because of fear and lack of knowledge and did nothing. A financial roadmap was put in place for her, and a solution was worked out that enabled her home to be saved. As she was leaving, she paused and turned and with tears in her eyes, said that she had made up her mind that if after the consultation there was no hope offered, she was going to go home and commit suicide, because everything had just become too much for her to bear…I was her angel.

Yes, it hurts every time you think of the departed, and it will continue to hurt, perhaps for a very long time or even forever. But life is for the living. Do you think that your loved one would be happy with you and the way you are acting? More likely not. Seek help from your church, from your doctor, someone trained in grief counseling. Your depression may be so deep that intensive therapy may be necessary. You can grieve; just don't continue to do it at your own expense.

**TAKE YOUR HEAD OUT THE SAND!**

# 4. Loss (Losing Your Home)

Due to sickness, loss of income (lay off or cut hours), a death in the family, poor financial planning etc., for whatever reason, you have gotten behind on your mortgage payments. Actually, you haven't made a payment in months. You are upside down in your home and you owe much, much more than what it is worth. Your neighbor across the street applied for a loan modification and a principal reduction and was denied, and their house is even bigger and nicer than yours. Why should you even waste your time applying, you are just going to be denied as well (see how our mind plays tricks on us), so why waste the time and effort. You've heard all the horror stories.

Meanwhile, the letters from the bank/mortgage company have just been piling up, all unopened. Why bother opening them, you know what they are going to say. The phone has also been ringing off the hook with calls from them. Two months creep by, three, four, five months and still you make no contact with the bank or any attempt to rectify the situation. Now the house is in foreclosure. You get an attorney that costs thousands of dollars to try to keep you in your home. Remember those letters that you didn't open that the bank sent you? You should have. In several of them were offers of a loan modification. The bank/ mortgage company were willing to work out a deal months ago with you but now it's too late. Or is it?

**TAKE YOUR HEAD OUT THE SAND!**

# 5. Battling Health Issues

It's been years since your last doctor's visit. Nothing major is wrong with you, just a little nagging pain here and there. Heart palpitations, small lump in the breast, shortness of breath, headaches, dizziness, blurred vision, indigestion, tingling sensation in the arms and legs to name a few. Cancer, diabetics, hypertension all run in your family. Doctors cost too much, and besides, you don't have any health insurance. Money is tight enough as it is without wasting it on going to the doctor when you know what they are going to say anyway! Unfortunately, a popular belief held by many is that if you go to the doctor, and they find something wrong with you, that's when you really die.

The reality of knowing that there is something wrong with you is less terrifying than the thought of knowing that something could be wrong with you. There are health clinics, programs at community organizations, churches set up to assist people with limited or no insurance. Check on the internet for additional information. In this instance, what you don't know can kill you!

**TAKE YOUR HEAD OUT THE SAND!**

# 6. Addiction

A dependency, physical or psychological, on a habit forming substance or activity that is detrimental to your wellbeing. What is your 'vice'? Alcohol, cigarettes, food, crack cocaine, heroin, gambling, prescription drugs, the list goes on and on. Anything ingested, injected, inhaled, inserted into the body, indulged in, in excess is an addiction.

Or, on the other hand, instead of being the addict yourself, you are an enabler. You don't necessarily actively encourage the destructive behavior but at the same time, nothing is being done to discourage/ eliminate it either. A lot of addicts are functional addicts. They are able to perform everyday tasks like go to work, and assimilate themselves into society without standing out and bringing attention to themselves. Take your classic alcoholic for example. He/she functions on the job and is able to maintain their performance level. But take a whiff/sip of that energy drink bottle they are always chugging!

An addiction is one of the toughest cycles to break. There has to be a realization on the part of the addict that help is necessary and a willingness to get the help needed. As for the enabler, help is necessary as well to cure the supportive behavior. Depending on the type of dependency, various groups exist that address the specific need. Check the internet for organizations in your area.

**TAKE YOUR HEAD OUT THE SAND!**

# 7. Overwhelming Financial Debt

Bills, bills, bills to pay, bills, bills every day! Sound familiar? The average American owes more in monthly bills than they make and take home. You know you are in serious financial trouble when you are using credit cards to pay for everyday expenses like groceries. All of your credit cards are over the limit, you have borrowed from everyone that would lend you money and you haven't paid them back and have no idea when or if you will be able to. You make only the minimum monthly payments (sometimes) on all your credit cards.

You are behind on the car payments and try to keep it locked in the garage so that the repo man can't get to it to repossess it. The stress from the situation is causing you to not sleep and your health is suffering. Every phone call is a creditor calling so you stop answering the telephone.

They are not going to go away. You will die and they will still be calling! Get on the phone and call all your creditors. If you feel that you can't do it yourself, get professional help. Go see a financial coach. If you decide that you can do it yourself, make arrangements with your creditors to get caught up with your payments. Try to negotiate a lower interest rate, transfer balances to another card. Display a willingness to deal with the situation.

**TAKE YOUR HEAD OUT THE SAND!**

# H.I.T.S.S. QUIZ

1. Do you not open mail when you receive it? **YES/No**

2. Do you avoid answering calls when you do not recognize the number displayed in caller ID? **YES/No**

3. Do you avoid dealing with situations? **YES/No**

4. Do you keep putting off completing important tasks? **YES/No**

5. Do you feel overwhelmed by situations? **YES/No**

If you have answered YES to at least one of the above questions, you may have H.I.T.S.S. syndrome.

# ACTION STEPS

Main factors to overcoming H.I.T.S.S. syndrome is:

- Acknowledge that a problem exists.
- Make a commitment with yourself to stop ignoring the issue.
- Identify people/persons, organizations that are able to assist you in solving your problem.

MOST IMPORTANTLY...

GET OVER YOURSELF AND ASK FOR THE HELP YOU NEED!!

TAKE YOUR HEAD OUT THE SAND!

## NOTES:

www.ingramcontent.com/pod-product-compliance
Lightning Source LLC
Chambersburg PA
CBHW060414080526
44583CB00012B/562